A BODY THAT REMEMBERS

♈

Poems By

Marcella Taylor

Art by

Patricia Canelake

Marcella
Christmas 2001

Black Hat Press
Box 12
Goodhue, Mn. 55027

2001

ISBN #1-88-7649-16-6

Acknowledgement is made to the following publications
in which some of these poems appeared: *A Rich, Salt Place,
A View from the Loft, Absorb the Colors, The Butterfly
Tree, Embers, Hurricane Alice, Intersections, Junction, The
Lost Daughter, The Lucid Stone, Poetry, Ragmag, Sisters
Today, Songs for the Arawak, Tampa Bay Review, Tremors,
Vibrations, Enough to Change the World, Wisconsin
Review.* Quotations from Dante's *Divine Comedy* are from
the English translation by Henry Wadsworth Longfellow.
The author would like to give special thanks to The Helene
Wurlitzer Foundation of New Mexico where many of these
poems were written.

Patricia Canelake: cover design from the painting, "Strange
Fruit" 2001, oil on paper (Duluth Public Arts, Technology
Village).

Book Design & Art: Ultramarine
www.patriciacanelake.com

Books may be ordered from:
Black Hat Press, Box 12, Goodhue, Mn. 55027
or from Amazon.com
or contact the author: taylormar@hotmail.com

CONTENTS

When in this wise she had her speech unloosed,
  She began to sing…

Dante, *Purgatorio*, xix, 16-17

For My Mother

GEMMA DONATI TO DANTE ALIGHIERI: LETTERS FROM FIRENZE

1.
Masses of stone push against this grille
closing my vision. Falsely shuttered towers
suffocate all that move beneath their shadows,
insects scurrying in a persistent twilight.
Only you who are no true lover have escaped.
Your letters boast of how you sit at table
refusing to be entertained by the coarseness
of a Verona court, rejecting with an arrogance
I am no longer permitted. I live as you do,
eating the bread of others but in my mouth
it has become dung. I even learn
to laugh when you are the butt of their jokes.
Forgive me,
I have no gift of words, nor grace of flesh.
I have only this. A mind that
walks where it will, a body that remembers.

2.
This night will move in like all others,
heat like a hunter attacking the valley.
Hesitant flares from one hundred towers
interrupt this world of black upon black.
A man sneaks off, my sleep slung over his back,
sleep that craves the burning of the hills.
Last week, a rider from Bologna described
the manuscript he saw, tales of crevices
filled with bodies, writhing in heat and mud.
The story, he said, tells of eternal punishment.
I say, No,
It is the earthly lot of those who see too much
and of those who share their bed without saying,
I love you.

3.

I vowed to halt this motion, like an aged bark,
upriver. I counted and sorted clothing, stored
food for the winter, then gathered the manuscripts
you left, stories of Job and Judith, arguments
of Aquinas, dog-eared pages from Tristan and Iseult,
records of Florence in happier days.
I read until the figures gyrated before my eyes,
refusing the struggle to form them into a city.
I left them in the eaves of the roof waiting
your return. I carried my body into the hills,
picked up a feather dropped by a huge bird,
graduated white to dark, wilting in the mud.
I stood content in the drizzling rain, caressing
hairs into fantastic shapes of my own making.

4.

Today, Ognissanti, the community shared bouquets,
flooded family tombs with their offerings. I woke
longing for your death enabling such a ritual, made
still the anger constricting my motion. I waited
till dusk, carrying blooms wrapped in a brown shawl
you bought for me on a sunny market day. Abreast
of the Alighieri houses, I stared uncomprehending
at the bundle in my arms. Alien voices floated out
of a high window forcing me into a ghostlike crawl
over stones. At Santa Margharita, my eyes fixed on
the Portinari tomb, shaking hands tore the shawl
away from the flowers, let them flutter over
pure marble. It seemed that Bea's fingers touched
my shoulder blades, steadied my trembling knees.

5.
From this tower, all is unseen but the churning
of the Arno. I fear being caught in an undertow.
With closed eyes, I concentrate on the scraping
of wheel against cobblestone. I too long to be
a ghost, haunting the air over a land we once
walked, arms playfully jostling each other.

6.
Down by Santa Maria Novella, my relatives gather
for a family portrait, wives, children, the men,
Corso's one living child growing sullenly
to an unmolested manhood.   I studied the face
of your enemy, noted how it mirrored mine, his
fleshy, mine growing gaunt and masculine, a tree
refusing to die. His voice was a falsetto,
your sons are gone, begging their livelihood
of their father's patron. You would not wish
your face etched in the annals of the city.
Nor the girl, startled like a fledgling
at any intrusion. I stumbled across flagstones,
too blind to see the Madonna in the niche,
the baby, face hidden, swaddled in stone.
Your face, my lover, molded in the workshop
of Giotto, must hold all memories safe.
We will become rock, each of us, make it easier
for generations to dream us back to life.

I

The dawn was vanquishing the matin hour
Which fled before it, so that from afar
I recognized the trembling of the sea.

Purgatorio, i, 115-117

WHATEVER WE DO

We meet again, wait again
for the canal to sing
loud enough for us to hear

for the church spires
to cast pointed lights
across our paths

my body feels nothing but
years become flesh, my voice
has lost its cadences

and you
have shaped your hair
finely against the skull

have found a place
in which to rest
each scorched leaf of life

when we repeat our old parting
nothing will have changed
no bird will drop a feather

whatever we do must be done
out of this void
we have both been carving

STILL LIFE

Discarding the list
of things to be done
I sit on the deck
in the steady light
of late morning

Earlier, in front of the mirror
I ran fingers over my cheeks
felt the barely perceptible ridges
carved out over the years,
trying to bury the false starts
of my life, the many dreams
seduced into being
only to be swiftly aborted

I became adept at that,
a cutting short of the wished for,
as if the excitement
was all in the wishing.
I tell myself

it is regret I should feel
but there are no clouds
to shadow this moment
to darken the sun bathing us all –

the boy who sits just inside
the window, eating contentedly
in front of the television,
the Siamese rising every few minutes
to rub her back against
my legs, the black cat basking
beneath the planter

the unmitigated light
melding it all together
on one single canvas.

AT THE ACOMA SKY CITY

Tales speak of movement from
up above to down below, gradual movement
of lives lived in layers on top of mesas,
the gradual descent from one level to another, until
the houses hugged the base of the cliffs
and the people no longer looked down with eyes
of gods on the dancers in the plaza below.

There are violent tales, too, a lightning storm
destroying the ladder that allowed Acoma ancestors
to come and go between flatland surrounding
the mesa and homes on the summit.
Only an old woman and her grandchild
were stranded on top. For four days
the clan circled the mesa, calling on the gods
to work the magic to bring them safely to earth.

It was not a time of blessings.
The two, hunger swelling their joints, clumsily
jumped to their deaths. The clan moved
to an adjoining mesa accustoming themselves
to the natural stone path leading to the summit
where burrows could be coaxed up
carrying their burden of water.

What I once saw held no faith in chants,
simply a roofer's apprentice, body curled up,
half spread across the stone path, half resting
on grass, a fallen roof ladder broken beside him.
He moaned, afraid to move, a neighbor bent
over him, paramedics soon swarmed the yard.
I greeted his boss, noted the rigid lines defining
his face. He set about cleaning up after
the day's work, not echoing my concern

over shattered bones, bleeding lifelines.
There would be no dance of healing.
In two days, the boy would return to work

When it was quiet and the cardinal returned
to the branch of the sycamore
to sing the evening in, I stood at the edge
of the yard, stared at the half-shingled roof
thinking of abandonment, of moving
far out of view of this scarred memory.
It was as if something had been desecrated,
some dream, some impossible hope
for the future, some form of expected arrival.

I did not know how to evoke
the magic language, or where to muster
the strength to make the break. Reluctantly,
I let the roofers complete their task,
sleeping amid auguries of fire and water.

The dreams waned as people started walking
the path where the body once lay, sitting
in chairs set out on the grass in circles, talking
and sipping beer as summer nights delayed
their darkening time and an alley light
illuminated the beans and tomato plants,
blooming daisies and marigolds.

Today, I stood at the edge of the mesa
that still housed the people. I looked down
upon the fields where beyond gathering,
crops danced in rows. My eyes
comfortably spanned the distance
to the ghost world, the enchanted mesa
where for centuries no one has walked.

I thought of the house ready for my return, how
it had become part of me, of apprehension
and despair, of continuances and blessings.
I purchased a small ceramic lizard, omen of trust,
listened while the potter explained the markings,
brown for earth,
white for rainbow, black for storms.

THE POTTER

Clay rises and swirls
under the pressure
of his hands. No,
it is the wheel
that gives it power
like a god coaxing it
to pivot slowly
into form, as a sorcerer
drawing out of the air
inhabitants of earth.

Those brown hands
that push upward
tensing the exterior,
fingers closing
together precisely
at the brim,
their task is only to
attend to the details,
the fine finishes
as in life
we hold onto only
a tiny piece
of the whole

letting the magic
wheel extend, expand
into the largeness
of our days.

MOVEMENT

You invited me, oh, so casually,
to join in the poker game
but none of life's experiences
prepared me for compromise

I pine for the sea
knowing all the time
it is less than a mile
from my front door

I am astonished at how life goes on
at how painlessly I flirt with
this one or that, at how nourished
by another's attention

It is as if I were resident
in some far off winter land
where night and day
overlap for hours

not here
where the sun drops
into the water
in an explosion of flame

and the stars that so swiftly
spatter the heavens seem so close
they will scorch your fingertips
if you stretch to touch them.

It is as if I want that winter land
without the aptitude
for moving so carelessly beyond
one moment to embrace another.

A HUNGER FOR RITUAL

It is March. The sun teases shining
bright and warm now and then,
but often receding behind clouds,
allowing cold winds and frost
to dominate the land.

It is midway to the solstice
when open air markets will be filled
with baskets of beans,
zucchini,
corn, spinach,
summer squash. The seed I planted indoors
must be tended daily. I wait for signs
of the first tiny sprout
making this my secret ritual.

Here in this cold city, I fear
to assume the boldness I covet,
to carry the new sprout through streets,
to say to the children, *Gaze at the power
of life,* and to the adults,
See how all will be well.

I dream myself into the village
of dead souls, making my ritual way
between shadowed buildings,
crying out to those who know
that such foolishness may yield blessings,
that fed
by our collective imaginations
we may awake into lives
where, despite the disturbance
of cycles, joy
will never desert us.

QUIET GATHERING

For a week with the family gone
I have tended the house,
cared for the things you loved.

Out in the back garden, tomatoes
burden the vines. Ripened,
they now lie fallen, juices spilled.

I gather those still leaning
from the vine, the pale orange,
the clear red. In the picking,

they overflow my hands. I make
a basket of the front of my skirt,
carry them into the waiting kitchen.

I pick a golden-petalled flower, dark
center intact, a single bloom
to keep me company through the night

in this house filled with the harvest
that outlived you, this house
now too silent, this house of rest.

ENGULFED IN WHITE

Driving along the highway, I move
into a world blowing white sheets across
invisible clotheslines. Nothing divides
January fields and roads. No sky overhead,
only a fading center island,
brief glimpses of overtaking vehicles.

It is years since I dared this
continuing to move in the face of death.
Impaired vision forces my foot
hard on the brake.

Alone, I am catapulted backwards.
Alone, I move from coast to plains,
from plains to everglades, driving
in rush hour traffic, circling big cities,
driving in a storm out of Duluth,
the single car on the road,
singing a forgotten song of rebirth,
all the way into the sun.

Now I lift my foot off the brake, move
into the outer lane, accelerate
to sixty miles an hour, drive
on a wantonly curving highway,
cocooned in violent snow, washing out
all semblance of darkness.

I am driving with vast midwestern
Spaces swimming on either side of me,
giving no edge to the cars
that follow in my wake,
driving into a world yet unborn.

MESSAGE TO MY NEPHEW IN PREP SCHOOL

Your voice came from a spot
where lakes and hills and plains intrude
upon each other. I was glad the contact
was finally made. You wanted me
to explicate a Dickinson poem. I was tied
to the practical affairs of life, neglected
to sing of the glistening fairyland
that woke me at dawn.

You had lived with me for four years then,
using the days to deepen your voice,
learn to fold your clothing, shut the door
of your room. You saw no reason
to phone each week. I would not explain.
I spoke only of how the poet floated
in language on planes
beyond absence, rejecting all subterfuge.

When I replaced the phone
in its cradle, I recalled the weekly epistles
that left the Green Ridge mountains
for turquoise waters where
Atlantic and Caribbean met. I was already
in college but just one year older than you.
I watched my first snow without pain,
yielded violin lessons for a place
on the hockey team, switched
roommates like clothing.

Tonight, evergreens are dark
against the snow and
the river moves over my flesh
without sound.

RECOVERY

The vendor sold me the shrimp,
fresh and pink. I carried them
in a smaller bag slung over one shoulder.
I shrunk against the wall,
anticipating vehicles that never passed.

You, my mother, waited behind a wall
that hid cooking paraphenalia
set out in front of the house, a family
homestead. I opened the larger bag,
poured out motley foodstuffs and weavings.

The smaller bag had disappeared.
I searched on earth
pressed down like concrete, on
dark old-fashioned counters,
in small sacks of garbage.

The shrimp did not matter, nor
my memory of their freshness
in the vendor's basket. Nor the fact
that in a blackened oven you kept
a store of virgin-like specimens.

What mattered was that
you had grown younger, that
gifted by the goddess who screens
visitors of the night, you
had recovered that erectness of body

a body that turned easily
in rhythm with the work
of your hands, my mind following
that rhythm without sorrow.

A DREAM OF WOLVES

I dreamt of wolves
how they entered the room
where the woman lay collapsed
how I was not able to keep them out
so shut them in with her
who lay still but breathing
on the floor
as if she and they were meant
to be yoked together.

I was not sure
then or later, that they were wolves
or needed to be feared, though here,
between my closed eyes, I clearly saw
their lean bodies, narrow snouts,
heard their howls, first
in the distance, then
in the room. The second howl
came from deep inside me.

I dreamt also of you
how we met again riddled
with memories we refused to share,
how you pulled me against you
body to body, mouth pressed against
the back of my neck, how
my whole body leaned into yours
as we stood unmoving at the door,
others passing in and out.

It all played out
on land and half-built structures filled
with strangers. The shadows
should have been more youthful here

in our old college town.
I could no longer navigate with ease.
Soon nothing was left but the wolves
and my own questions
about what I had seen and heard.

In that first instance of waking
I smiled in remembrance
of the joy of a mended love, a promise
that the years of wisdom
might not be lonely.

I also recalled that
I found the old woman unconscious
on the floor, the wolves moving in,
only because I thought it was
your hand begging me to enter.

CHASING THE DREAMS

In this log cottage, I watch morning light
enter, lean my head against pillows, delay
the day's start. I reach for the dream,
its treasury of images forming
mosaics of sleep now fading into shadows,

houses, clothing, colors and tones
swiftly yielding to the next, a fluid motion
propelling me into this waking,
waiting to be moved this way and that
by the entrances of others.

It is the house of the soul I beg
to inhabit, clothing once cherished
I pray to enfold me. Even
the sun's reflection is darkened
by what lies in the way—

Chair, lamp, the painting achieved
against a closet door,
an abstract mass of dark and lights,
the wren's song outside the window,
a series of pauses, recapitulations.

It is the forgotten plazas
of dreaming
that I would lay down
with the thoughtfulness of an artisan
stone by stone.

II

We at the point were where no more ascends
The stairway upward, and were motionless,
Even as a ship, which at the shore arrives.

Purgatorio, xvii, 76-78

ANOTHER TIME, A DIFFERENT PLACE

I watch the news, the Serbs refusing
to move heavy weapons from the walls
around Sarajevo, ready to endure
mutual bombardment, rather than jettison
the work of "ethic cleansing."
Every time I see the leader's face,

I see you, brown hair, solid figure, recalling
that summer when we met so easily
on a Cambridge street. I knew little of your world
then, only that it had been held together
by a man called *Tito,* that in some drab
postwar building you taught French verbs.

After we had coffee
in a Brattle street café, I agreed
to meet you at some foreign film,
a Fellini perhaps, or a Resnais, figures
to lead us boldly
beyond a romantic world.

I never got there. Walking across
the Commons, caught in a deluge,
I was appalled at my drenched body,
my hair gone limp, my sallowed face.
I headed for Roxbury Crossing,
my small transient apartment.

I stripped bare to dry myself,
then sat staring onto a narrow street.
It was too late for the voices
of children playing
down below. I saw only
a barren landscape of late afternoon.

Did you wait for me? Did you think
that in some careless moment
I went off with someone else? It was
not like that. Each man I met that summer,
the ex-priest, the Tunisian, the mandolin player
was given my full attention.

All we had were names
(now I have forgotten yours),
no numbers, no streets. The times
were just so, overcasual meetings succeeded
precipitously by separations, the failure
to take time to shape and meld,

to communicate more deeply
who we were, what elated us, what events
might suddenly make our angers rise.

Now I catch myself hating your kind,
in my heart calling you Nazi.
No, not you.   I still see your eyes
light up, your hand move softly over
my face, as if you were smoothing out
a sculpture you had chiseled

your voice chanting an ode
to my voice, my walk, your gestures
saying how
ethnic differences didn't matter.
It is often thus when
two people meet face to face.

TELEPHONE VOICE

When his voice came over the wires
A voice I could no longer pick out of a crowd

A voice of casual moments
Swayed by the loveliness of leaves

The flow of architecture
The delicacy of water and glass

When through the passing of years
There came to me this chord of remembrance

I turned back
Not to that childhood solitude
Lying on a porch
My back to the sapodilla tree

Dreaming a world I knew could not exist
Instead I recalled how my body swelled

And needing more space began
To sweep a path this way and that

Began to mail letters without return addresses
Began to lease rooms without doors

When I heard cocooned in words
What the hand could hold

I made my body pause still afraid
No matter what it had just learned

I held my limbs still not ready yet
To let the heart explode.

IN A HOLDING PLACE

In the early twenties, my mother
stole the streets of Miami,
squinting through mammoth windows
at manikins with false eyelashes.

A slim young woman whose tawny skin
cocooned hues of desire,
she stormed the libraries for tales
containing words for life—

ardor, zest, gusto
flame, passion, spirit
breath, energy, vivacity
tumult, bustle, sweat
chagrin, anguish, extremity
acedia, torpor, somnolence

At sunset, she returned to eat
in a house that like a chasm
separated homes of black and white.

When the parlors were
faintly illuminated, roadhouses
came alive and black dancers swished
satin costumes with lizard-like ease

but my mother sat
in a straight-backed chair
reciting the words to herself,
storing them one by one so that

when the time came
at the sound of her voice
they would awaken.

ARCS

Now the pleasures come
not like the sun appearing before
the halt of the rain, but like
the first leaves of spring expected, waited for
in painful emergence from the branch.
Or like the payday
with the money already parceled out,
the rent, the utilities,
the half-empty grocery bags.

Frantically, I shuffle the pages
layering my life, minutes that hushed
the excited cries of childhood,
gold stars and badges sucking in mildew
in some far recess of the body.

If joy had been squeezed
to a skeleton beneath the explosions
of life, if too many roman candles
release only a fraction of their light,
if the earth so filled with tremors
refuses these crescents
that will never become faces,

how can we learn to live where
both light and shadow frame us,
where our fingers cannot caress
the tops of the trees

how are we gifted to open
the door on our pain
in these weeks of birthing,
how let the tiniest color explode
full strength beneath our skins.

WORDS FOR THE CHILDREN
OF THE FUTURE

There was a time when fire
Was used for more than destruction
When those who moved about
In brick buildings
Craved warmth and light
And found ways to control the fire
And sustain it. Once

We sat around the table
In the semi-dark
And the white candles
Curled their edges
Toward their cores where
Black wicks leaned into the air.

Each flame was not a fixed thing.
It wove back and forth, broadening
Then narrowing its perimeters
At will, now pushing itself
Horizontally outward, now reaching
For the ceiling.

Later
When the room where we sat
And rooms everywhere were sucked
Into the fluted edges
Of a mushroom artifact, those
Whose bodies suffered only changes
In shape and texture
Looked frantically for the candles
They knew had been stored
Against such a day. They looked
Deep down in drawers

Where they had placed their green
And crimson and yellow wax forms,
Some tapering,
Some so firm and rounded
They needed nothing for balance.

These survivors
Were horrified to find
Only gray globs of matter
Which sucked to blackness
The flames from flaring matches,
Flares that lasted only an instant.

And when we sat there
In a time now hard to imagine
We thought our words were candles
We thought our poems
Were the sustainment of life
We thought what we fabricated

Would be lasting monuments
To human love.

IN A PARIS METRO STATION

I catch a glimpse of the body
lying on the other track
as the train slows to a stop.
I say nothing. I am used to deaths
I have no energy left to mourn,
departures that now go unremarked.
The man who made that flying leap
is no doubt still alive.
Our train stops, unloads
and loads tired, hopeful bodies.

We will move on, leave the man
lying there, waiting for
the oncoming train. We will move,
leave the passengers
on the opposite platform waiting
for the ride to take them into
the names we have already lived.
The doors close

But now
people are crowding
the windows,
the lights go out,
the doors open.

We cannot continue the journey.
We are forced to join hands
in ignorance
with this nameless tragedy
that lies still and breathing
in a world persistently
moving us backwards.

WINTERING IN BORROWED TERRITORY

You have become used to avoiding crowds
since autumn swallowed your shoeprints
on the grass. You sip coffee, watch sparrows
crowd the feeder, flakes that fall in no hurry
to reach the ground. You did not put that feeder
in place. It is not your window.
And the fine variations in the feather of the chickadee
communicate nothing to you. Even
the coffee is brewed in someone else's pot.

You have become used to this solitary ritual,
the clock's hands silently pointing to midnight,
the easing down of the calendar, the one
filled with kittens in the illusion of stillness.
You pause in your task, glance
into the small mirror over the sink,
wondering about patience, about
what they say, how social revolution
does not take place in one generation.
                              Sometimes
you would be willing to embrace the rhythm
of unshod feet, the fingers where skin hugs bone,
the fingers that clutch knives and guns,
weakness from hunger that topples ancient stone.

You find the new calendar, the one that marks
each month in prairies and half-grown trees
and rocks not yet smooth. On at least one page,
you decide, there must be a young bird trying
to sing a song, a note that reincarnates a tune
no living thing can remember. But
you do not turn the pages. Patience, you say
to yourself. You hang it cautiously on one wall
of the rented kitchen. You dream once more

of your voice locked in summers
you once thought you owned, how it will shatter
the glass separating the seasons. You ignore
the blood on the cheek as you clutch
the polished stone in the palm of your hand.

STITCHES

It begins garbed in innocence.
First they say,
We will seal the document
to protect the health of the country.

Then they announce,
Here is the story. What has been
omitted will not be understood
except by the initiated.

Later,
they will gather the reporters
in a room without windows and say,
Here are the pictures.

Each time we give a signal,
Play them over and over again,
The people will have become children,
They will not know the difference.

As for the asylums, we will send
the inmates out on the street
to beg and die of exposure
when that neverending winter arrives.

But they keep the edifices intact
and waiting
for those who long
to see the sun again

Who one morning awake
and begin to struggle without hands
to remove
the stitches from the eyelids.

THE LOVER-GENERAL

One the red cover
of the newsmagazine, he is proclaimed
the sexiest man in America. He tells them
when to fire and when to hold fire.
If it were up to him, he would have
marched forward until not one fresh breeze
found its way into the desert.

The media appropriates the voice
of the females of the land,
describing how at night we toss and turn,
bodies aflamed, groping in sleep
for the folds of his face, the blurred
angles of the body,
the dark power over life and death.

The men are jealous, afraid.
Like Uriah, they will be placed
on the front lines while
the women are fed to the general,
strengthening his resolve.

Will these women soon neglect
their work, their children, their music,
reaching out only to experience
the orgasmic heat shooting
down the years, making
world upon world collapse in his arms.

SOS

Thinking you had received
a reward, this walk forward
to a city scarcely visible
in the yellow lamps of morning

and thinking
you would walk it
burdened only by the years
half-consciously gathered

and ready
to move alone
but open to brief interludes
with other travelers

this phone call
comes
like a blow to the stomach
in a dark room

You know how
the wallet had become flattened
how urgent the tick of the clock
with the passing years

You feel more sharply than ever
the injured shoulder, the constant
back pain, an ankle
that won't heal, arthritic hands

that no longer grasp with confidence
Yet you listen to yourself
calmly say the words
to reassure the family

You place the telephone in its cradle
turn your face towards the city
see its river making diamonds
in the midmorning light

You can hear the exchanges
in the cafes the soundtracks
of the theatres
the music in the metro

You think perhaps you can touch
the thorns on the rosebushes
in the park

You wonder
how you can steel yourself
against desires crowding in

how
you can make your feet retrace
their steps into a waiting tunnel

how
you can freeze the motions of the body
without turning into ice.

FAILED RENDEZVOUS

It was a road I refused even before
we met, your eyes dark and welcoming,
my gestures spontaneous despite myself.
It was as if we were walking a path

and the spring leaves of trees bent
to brush my cheek, passing on the breezes
that impelled them. You lived in Milan,
city fecund with remade shapes, the music

of love. I inhabited Florence, a world
of scaffolding and dust. It was the promise,
a Rome meeting, where stone gods would hurl
back the sounds we had almost lost.

Like crockery falling in a vacuum,
I took care of things. I was used to betrayal,
a hatred of the mirror's false flesh.
This hot valley was my place. I focused

on escaping death in traffic, on faded
frescoes, on faces that looked only inward.
I could imagine your eyes
scanning the room, my absence waiting

to make a myth of something
that would lie buried, evocative.
Better than presence, a dish
glued together, the surfaces uneven,

the meeting point streaked,
cracks pulling darkness through.

ARES

This is not the god of war
we know today, this quiet figure
with the pensive human face.

The limbs sport
no angularity, the flesh
no curves that define motion.

No doubt, the battle was a draw,
it not being clear on which side
the writhing bodies belonged.

Had the god stayed
away from Olympus too long,
forgetting the taste of nectar?

For twenty centuries now
he has been forced to listen to
the insistent revolution of earth.

He has shut out the clang
of iron against flesh
by rooting himself in stone.

III

We were still on the border of the sea,
Like people who are thinking of their road,
Who go in heart but in the body stay.

Purgatorio, ii, 10-12

NAKED BEACH

The true places of beauty
on the island
are left lonely, deserted

like this beach

the narrow but pristine stretch
of sand
snaking beside the water

the water itself
green and translucent
all the way to the curved horizon

palms shading tufts of grass

the waves' incessant rhythm
as they lick the shore
edging towards the rocks

where we may sit tall
as if
we were the first
to people the earth

FACULTY PICNIC

Despite hayrides to distract them,
the children were always underfoot
like baby kittens. The older ones
reached out to subdue the younger
who pulled away
in rosy-cheeked rebellion. A tiny poodle
searched for a ball not lost.

We choked on the smoke
of the open fire and the hotdogs
burned and the pop was tepid,
But the beer iced the throat,
the potato chips crisp
and brownies neither soggy nor
like rock.

When the clearing away began
and the voices got louder, I escaped,
sat alone by the water, welcoming
the sound of an outboard motor
drowning out all else. I watched
the lake water churn heavily
in the wake of the craft

and remembered the landscape
of water and song I once tried
to dream into being. I did not wait
like the others
for the setting of the sun
to start the drive home.
I did not need the fading light.

A WALK DOWN DIVISION STREET

The water hides behind buildings,
emerges only at five corners,
singing behind railings
to morning walkers, whispering
answers to the secret air.

The bank is dressed in weekend
nudity. The jeweler has taken
a coffee break. His assistant
with the one-eyed glass
smiles at my disintegrating frames.

He mumbles of nuts
and threading. I stand
at a half-angle moving into
blindness, fingering figures
back into existence.

Down the block, I pass over
exposed cartridges, reflections
of unrecalled movements, caring
but slightly which gestures
are captured, which lost.

Neutral stills
now speak louder,
moments held and passed,
redeemed acts frozen,
silhouetted into being.

In the bookstore, I flit
from Jung to Lessing, shuffle pages
of Mother Earth, seek for the right binder
to hold fleeting minutes,

find nothing, possess nothing.

The way home gradually slopes,
Leaves the river no glances,
no regrets.
The day is the last
of Indian summer surviving itself.

Tomorrow, thawed ice
will seep through the mats, winter
will struggle to seal out the dew.
We will delay moving the door back
on its hinges, try to capture

these days, these streets,
these moments of stasis, these
black and white dreams.

HERON

The peach sunset
stretched across
the nine o'clock sky,
reaches down,
cooling the still
shallow waters
of the lake.

A blue heron,
tall-legged,
perched on a rock,
then flew low,
strong wings spread
wide.

We held our breath
till he was out of sight
and wingless,
saddled our dreams
and moved on.

LEGACY

The older woman spends the days
In sisterhood, laying forks
Out on a table on the back porch,
Climbing into passenger seats
For a trip to the city, absorbing
Fantasies in darkened theaters.

If you let the mirror call forth
Her presence, you will find her
Talking, smiling, laughing
As before, when years stretched
Ahead of the two of them,
A purple road with white hills.

The younger woman moves
Aimlessly through the rooms,
Pausing only to open cupboards,
Unearth manuscripts, discover
A cranny in the cellar
Filled with rejected ceramic pots.

With his words clutched between
Her fingers, she takes a walk
As if blue ink will reveal what
Was held back through the years,
A father she tentatively touched,
A man she can no longer hold close.

The widow stares at the pots
Her daughter bears on a tray,
Wondering softly if
This is the moment she can
Allow herself to let go.

FLOWERS FOR CHARLIE

All in girlish white I sat stiffly
at a table in the bar
not sure what to order.
You smiled, a handsome glint
in your blue eyes, ready
to follow my lead.

The other two settled
for beers, we dared the cocktail.
You were my first college date
and I was too young.
Why am I remembering you
tonight, decades later?

Is it the figure of my silence,
the awkwardness of my feet
the fear of showing
how proud I felt
to have been matched with
the catch of the college town?

The hall was a film of floating
shadows, the music silenced
after our second dance,
our midnight goodbyes
at the convent dorm tentative.
You were off to the army

and only now
with all the miles between
this room and the men
I still love,
am I wondering
if you made it back alive?

WAKING TO THE SOUND OF RAIN

I dreamed of your bathroom
in precise detail, bottles
flooding porcelain
surfaces, glass shelves.
A large green towel draped
over the bathtub's rim.

I berated myself
for not tidying it, woke
into a universe of rain
that would wash away
the footprints on the deck
overlooking the bay

woke into a floating in water
without a lifeline to connect
flesh with the blossoming world.
I had slept fitfully, shifting
to give my eyes time
to merge with sea shadows.

The harvest of three nights
when I waked to your presence
bathed me in the stability
of the enwombed, a gift
to be nourished, to put on hold
these days of floating alone.

STILLPOINT

Tourists skirt dead fish
lying on the dock, marble eyes
fixed by the noonday sun,

climb into mole-shaped craft,
sink hips below water, ready
to sight bloom of the depths.

Waters separate. Fish and flora
dance multicolored before
their eyes, tracing flesh encased

in glass, voices echoing
like murmurs of the entombed.
It is only the diver

in the quiescence of motion
who desires the naked self
or body mottled by disease

twisted by foreign habitation
that glimpses the tunnel
in the ocean bottom.

Flesh learns its lesson well,
stifles the cry against
disenfranchisement, lets

an arm drop heavily into air.
At the still point of the water
the diver pauses before the ascent,

opens the cage she carries, releases
fish rainbowed by the surface.

PENINSULA

I remember white ocean water
hesitantly showering
a glassy spray
over knife-tipped rocks

and I recall too how the land
always curved itself,
coming to a point
too far from shore to be seen

and when the sun went down
how we had to gather
each piece of clothing, pulling it
over our half-dried bodies

Our eyes were always
turned backwards
as we headed for the car
I slept all the way home then

not knowing about pirate tortures
or wild packs of dogs
that once roamed the shores
I slept without waking

not knowing the later generation
who might look at those waters
to see only the sun
exploding into their depths, witness

the slashing of delicate skins,
the earth become arid
and the people left alive
who would stand

shading with fins
the hollows that were eyes,
searching for a glimpse
of that tip of the land

which I as a child
loved having to imagine.

THE ROWERS

Down below
tiny rubber craft
are steered by double oars,
some alone struggling
for balance
in recalcitrant waves

others in pairs
learning to dip and lift
dip and lift
together

while above
without need of hands
I sit in a cradle,
the meetingpoint
of a double tree trunk, all
rounds and crooked curves

taking me back
to my child's body
with white stones piled
high in mounds
sustaining me there.

ELEGY FOR A CITY

In Venice
soft green carpets support the buildings
yielding to the waters
that cradle them. Holiday-makers
turn the streets
into a world of orgy. Each delays the retreat
indoors, shops refuse to close.

The ferryboats
continue to carry full loads
of passengers the length of the main canal
throughout the night. The crowds
on the bridge use time exposures
to imprint for posterity
the artificial lights playing on the water.

When the darkness
captures the city, the black
gondolas will sneak through
the smaller waterways, the songs
of the boatmen echoing
like the toll
of church bells from the mainland.

MOTHER AND CHILD

I was sleeping away from home
the night you died waiting
for the ambulance to arrive.

My sister's car idled
in the carport
as if fate demanded a delay,
insisting there be no false breathing
to write your epilogue.

They say
you easily saw death enter,
showed no fear, calmly
handing out admonitions
to the living. Outside,

it was
a clear tropical night, perhaps
a late rising moon that gradually
spread a green glow

over coconut palms
that shaded your bedroom
and the garden plot
where you spent the day weeding.

At least, that's the way
I imagine it,
your soul wrapped
in that ethereal light, freed
of arthritic pain and failing memory.

I do not really know.
There was no outer darkness

in that noon hour
when the message reached me.

The darkness was laid out
within me, locked in place
waiting to stalk me
through the months that followed

not letting me sever my being
from the shadow you left behind,

half of our twin selves
entering the world of death,
the other half
left behind to roam the earth.

TARANTULA

When I spied the creature
hugging the bedroom doorpost,
it looked so elegant, boasting
furred black legs.
It did not seem to belong to nature.
When it moved, we attacked it
with the deadly spray. It began
a climb upward against
the closet door. I fetched the broom,
brought it down hard on its back.

Its legs spread wider,
turned inward, beginning
a slow journey towards the floor,
seeking perhaps
some crevice for sanctuary.
Its legs had become gaunt,
elongated and narrow,
as it crawled toward me.
Was it begging pity?
Fear moved me
to lift its body with the bristles
of the broom, fling it against the wall.

It landed on the floor, legs
curled crossing over one another,
resembling dried seaweed.
We swept it down the hall,
through the living room, across
the porch, into the yard.

It lay there
charcoal and shriveled.

Death is terrible, no matter
the cause. I soothed myself,
imagining its fatal sting.
Must it always happen
like this, the deadly contest,
one left to breathe, the other
to shrivel and die?

We stood
at the door in silence
watching the night swallow
sea and land. I thought,
It wouldn't have been so bad
if in dying
it could have retained
its velvet beauty.

BITS OF NATURE

Walking these sandy beaches
we cannot escape attack.

Small brown particles fasten
our clothing into bundles.
The soles of our feet
and the palms of our hands
are pierced by slivers of wood.

Even if we begin
to wear shoes
our bodies
will enclose souvenirs
of daytime dreams.

We move our eyes over
a horizon thick with color,
praying we may be blessed
to carry these shapes
to plains far from the sea.

These winds
that twist our garments
will reach the mainland
drained too soon
of the smell of salt.

We must be ambassadors
deputized to preserve
the residue
of this land secure
beneath our skins.

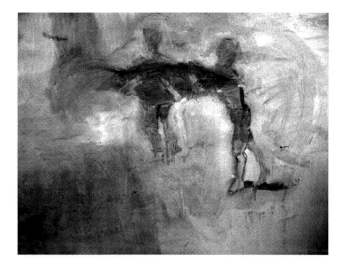

IV

Along the solitary plain we went
As one who unto the lost road returns,
And till he finds it seems to go in vain.

Purgatorio, ii, 118-120

RESUMING THE JOURNEY

I loved sitting there
at only a slight distance from
those slender bay windows, the huge elm
outside brushing against brownstone walls.
Moses, the middle cat, would perch
on the window seat watching
squirrels and birds
in a rare moment of contentment.

I made a place inside me for
that shelter, its elegant white walls,
spotless marble fixtures, gallery lights.
I liked its flow of open spaces,
the sun entering and traveling
from one room to another
unimpeded.
The cats rolled across carpets
together, forming dual and triple bonds.
At times, I felt like an outsider.

Even there.
I let those light-filled
rooms in but kept myself out, travelling
from day to day
as if in a convoluted tunnel,
waiting for a point of arrival.

I wrote in my journal,
I will make these spaces my own
when I discard alien alliances,
the only fruit of a beleaguered life.
This place that touched my being
I could not own
for I did not own myself.

I sold it to a couple
who would divide their time between
this city place and a river house,
who in that division
would meld body and space.

I packed the furniture
which fit only with great unease
into other rooms, bundled the cats
into carriers without bars. We started
on our way, moving from
place to place, their sustainment
the familiar smells of each other,
mine only the journey itself.

PARTING THE COUNTRYSIDE

The sun climbs far above the grass,
Campers start their motors, push off
For the day's tour. They exit
By the far left lane. Caravans line
On the right, waiting for gates to open.

The fields are strangely naked.
Twenty-odd ponies cluster
On a roadway island, torsos brushing,
Eyes begging nothing, limbs lacking
The domestic mare's restless shuffle.

Along the road, a white pony and colt
Come in single file, forepaws lifted
At each step. They appropriate the lane
Marked for those bearing permits.
As we drive forward to seek the road out,

I remark how no pony stands isolated
this morning. Even the cattle rest huddled.
Calves lean against mothers' flanks.
Black and gray bodies extend over the field's edge,
Calm eyes stare through cruising cars.

My companion is unmoved by the scene,
Fails to acknowledge my dismay
Over our break with the earth. We travel
Against the sun, going
Where those with native claims

To the land must again and again
face, behind the dusk
of concrete walls, this passive
invasion of the plains.

IN THE NEW FOREST

Colts stretch their bodies beneath
the forelegs of adult ponies.
Feathered creatures are silenced
by the chirp of their young.
Calves totter, lift their necks
to suck warmth from their mothers.

A thousand years ago these lands
were pruned to satisfy royal pleasure.
Today, the queen's huntsman
disclaims the right to breed
new deserts. In summer, the park
is repossessed for the future.

Eyes of children solemnly follow
fingers that point out
objects revealed in the rising sun.
Each day I walk to hear the echoes
of the invisible forest creatures, cries
resounding the first breath of life.

Down the road
in the village of Burley, children
pour into the streets, watch
parent ponies stroll their colts
through heavy traffic.
They stand them

at the entrance to a delicatessen
teaching them to grasp
their inheritance without timidity.

PRUNING THE GARDEN

He climbs the steps to my front porch.
Eagerly, I go to meet him, the tall man
with dirt-stained palms who promises
to bring abundance to my garden.

The sky is slightly overcast, the rain
has stopped falling, the sun emits
faint light to guide our steps over
weed-infested grass, gray stone paths.

He points out plants that need uprooting,
limbs that need pruning, the earth
that cries out for nutrients. Standing
in front of the stone slab retaining wall,

he tells me what I feared, that
the evergreen shrubs turned rust
in the ice-storms of winter must go.
No amount of care will revive them.

I wonder what will replace them. I turn
my head to face north, away from
the garden, reflecting how easily
things die, how hard it is to find seeds

to get life moving again. The warm days
are more than half over and winter rises
before my eyes. But I turn back to face
the sun, to listen to his explanation,

what plants will still bloom, and how,
in the shade of the overhanging tree
where grass refuses to endure, flowers
may still flourish before the frost.

We come to the vegetable bed where,
on hands and knees, I eradicated all growth,
all that was weed and choking
which may still arise. There, he says,

peat moss and cattle compost mixed
with the depleted soil will do the job.
Onions, radishes, beans may spring up.
Earth does not yield its right to nourish.

CONTINUITY

In the square outside the Uffizi
the Medici heads and Preraphaelite faces
are echoed. These women
project an angular delicacy

like no other nation. They walk
in their elegant unobtrusive clothing
ignoring the hunger in the Mediterranean eyes
that follow them. They are

both ruler and models. Their high-heeled
boots tap the stone
surfaces. With roman noses
they sniff out the future

where still the crowds descend
upon the city to stare at
the numerous Madonnas and complain
that they are not Jewish.

PASSION FOR LIGHT: VINCENT VAN GOGH

Wanting a world light-flooded
he preached in the snows,
calloused hands hanging awkwardly
from rough wooden sleeves.

Wanting a world light-flooded
he moved south where strong winds
buffeted his canvases causing
the colors to bleed in pain.

Wanting a world light-flooded
he dreamed of a childhood lived
by the canals, and a god
whispering out of a pale blue sky.

Wanting a world light-flooded
he lay aside figures
of sheep, to paint love
with withered breasts.

Wanting a world light-flooded
he worshipped the painter who
in the dark hues of Tahiti evoked
a world that refused to visit him.

Wanting a world light-flooded
he walked out into the fields
and aimed at the crows
that darkened his breasts.

VAN GOGH, *FLYING OVER CORNFIELDS*

Stalks of corn shot up
Out of the earth, some yellow,
alive with joy, others
clutching the heat of age,
brown with spent fury.

The sky, washed by sun,
cuddled trees
bedded against the horizon.
Paths, late summer green
invited his feet to walk softly

but when he lifted his brush,
the flesh trembled, the path
blossomed brown patches
and his soul
became the invisible earth.

Then
the black ravens moved in,
sky turned over dark blue
swallowing outer branches of trees,
cornstalks shuddered
in the wind, bent bodies eastward.

Still the ravens
skimmed with bravado
overhead
loud cries echoing backwards
towards an unpainted world

where the sun
ducked for cover.

VAN GOGH, *BANK OF A RIVER WITH ROWING-BOAT AT ANVERS*

Leaves dancing over the edge
of the land, making mirrors
in the narrow gullies
between brightly-painted boats,
women with full bosoms, jaunty hats,
a sail ready to list in the wind.

Perhaps something else, a moment
touched by what always eluded him
like a single shaft of light
across the bathroom floor, a half-
rainbow as the day cleared
or else a visit from his brother.

Whatever it was,
he almost resurrected its name,
there
in the surface of the water

where all the bright colors
of his palette wove
a slender thread
to catch and hold for an instant
the spinning earth in his palm.

LEAVING THE HOUSE

The house leans towards the river
as if to ignore my plans for betrayal.
The woman talks of a stair curved here,
a fire door placed there, a hot water heater
moved adjacent to the furnace,
a closet transformed into a study.

Out on the driveway we smell
the first breeze of spring. The snow
has gone except for ugly patches
rising in small hills. The lawn
is a swamp, the ice-dotted waters
move fast eating up the flatter banks.

My smile hides little.
I can say goodbye with ease, fail
to fulfill all the promises
I made to myself and this land
without bitterness. I said
it would be a marriage. Together
we would nurture each other

grass and flesh caress as one
the days that stretch
to become the fat of years.

Lives are like that. The flower
thinks it will grow and grow, outlast
the impatient northern summer.
It dies in a day, or if born under
a lucky sign, a week, drops its seed,
receives new life in different earth.

As I wave them off,
buyer and friend, I can already feel
March days turning back to winter,
the sun failing below
the overpass, the cars hushing
their motors.   I turn indoors
feeling nothing except
the enclosure of a temporary swamp.

SILENCE AT SUNSET

You turn the car away
from the mountains,
park where one can see
only a deep valley
filled with artifacts
of a transient world.

I can admire the houses
nestled here, imagine life
moving forward
while mountains rise
beyond sight of it all.
But what I truly spy

are the colors
we turn our backs on
how they shift hour by hour
red to purple to blue.
I keep silent about it all,
keep my desires stifled,

how we would move
beyond this, the valley life
imprisoning us
how we might grow
eyes at the backs
of our heads,

understand how
such life and death changes
are paintings
of the sun
going to bed with its love
the earth.

VISTA IN JOLIET

Down by a strange dirt-filled shore
Elders from old world countries
Fill their garden with virgin shrines
Lit by red petals.
The houses all look toward the water
Hidden from view by trees
That breathe contaminated air.

A few streets away
The dark faces of the new world
Loiter on sidewalks
Marked with lines of unpacked
Cartons. They shade their eyes
To see beyond the faded brick
That blocks their view.

THE UNWANTED VISITOR

For a week my big toe battled
the freeing of its nail. Now
a new covering spreads,
incomplete, crooked, half-raised.

I walk between my unmade bed
and the clutter of papers, ignoring
the mirror that has forgotten
the virginal forms.

Day after day
I avoid the sight
of this grotesque creature
that embeds itself into my flesh.

The trees fed by the angry rains
exude a richer green
so that we almost taste it.
The earth says, I will be
planted once more
and then again. The children
squeal in unconcern.

Only
their parents frown
to see the leather tightening
around their feet, the dresses
that yield to thrusting hips.

It is more than a toenail
shriveled with the knowledge
of the disaster of years.
The summer is filled with the drone
of invading insects.

The ghost of my future appears
more frequently, wrinkled and deformed.
It enters without ceremony
points with laughter
to the parallel lines that boldly
curve across my neck, the furrows
that rise between the eyes.

Even the hills turn hostile
become a threat to gentle breathing.

At least once a year
the trees splinter in the winds,
the fields are given over
to the nurturing of hay
waiting for autumn cuttings.

I lose myself
in late summer
trying to find a path
in the middle of such disorder.

I go with naked feet
I climb the hills in stages
I enter my house without knocking

V

And of that second kingdom I will sing
Wherein the human spirit doth purge itself,
And to ascend to heaven doth becometh worthy.

Purgatorio, i, 4-6

NAMING THE SELF

1.

As a child, I loved to skip puddles
in the Public Market where turtles
doomed to death lay in tubs.
I fantasized myself such a creature,
accepting that burden tight against my back,
unable to hug anything close to my bosom.

2.

Within me, the races of my country gather,
a country of late arrivals, a wishing star
for the hopeless. I no longer live there,
prefer truck stops, walks in alien fields
where I may go unrecognized. At night,
I scan skies, search out the selfsame star.

3.

In a strange land, I make random purchases –
Indian rattle, drum, a round dance shawl,
Navaho earrings, piñon incense
in the shape of a *kiva*. I lay them in drawers,
beneath the bed, fear to bring them forth,
fear to learn what they know of spirit.

4.
Birds here avoid the sky. They cry aged cries,
joust at the edges of splintering branches
touch ground to chase intruders. Against
black bodies wings red or white seldom fold.
A restless breed, they refuse
to sever themselves from things of earth.

5.

Wires carry messages that imprison. Blood
flowing as one constricts movement.
Book, bird song, cloud filament make no
difference. I tiptoe the living voices
of the gorge, swim dried up bed, twist self
four-sided. Odd side reflects a liquid moon.

6.

First sun, steps go as blood directs. Eyes
focus where brain leads. Animals know
when to arrive, how to sit quiet. Pages
flutter at fingertips' command. Heart marches
to an unspoken rhythm. *Second sun*,
whirling dance in a black wind. Obedience.

7.

The crystal forms its own graph. We use it
for contemplation but see only our faces,
lines etched like ghost rubbings. We think
glass might do better, how it holds whatever
escapes us, how it shatters on command.
We like forgetting. We like being made brittle.

8.

Take them all and hold them. Earth, rock,
sky, paper, corn, table. Turn them over.
Put this letter in that place. Move them all
toward nothing but shapes, lines, tracings.
Package them. Hand them over saying, *Here is
what has become of me. It is now yours.*

9.

The wren paces below my window.
Long-tailed, rust-breasted, brown-feathered,
it reminds me of nothing. If ravens cry out,
it is absent. If wolves rush by, its presence
is only the interstices of their howling.
It enters no dreams, can easily be ignored.

10.

Youths roam byways of the dead city,
smashing windows long since removed.
The ghost car of a cop sits in a field, once
a parking lot. Aping the crumbling of steel,
they imagine a new star. At dawn, they bury
bodies beneath gestures. No one can name them.

11.

Spiders journey toward flesh. Oblong wings
wait at entrances. When attacked with words,
ants curl bodies inward. Magpies eat death
of their own kind. Clouds bed atop mountains.
Eyes grow over our bodies. When mirrors
spring from seed, only one remains closed.

12.

I move from place to place, fingering textures
woven into heat. I own nothing but what fits
on my back. My skin is tattooed with footprints.
At dark, I speak into a machine not yet invented.
I do not know myself in a new city. The earth
is the only one who recognizes my name.

WITHOUT FEAR

I watch a magpie swooping
in the field to my right
stealing away my gaze
from the faint layers of snow
still draping distant mountains.

Four years ago, I saw a pair
nest in the trees on the grounds
of my small cottage, pushing
chunky bodies of their young
out of the nests, forcing them
to discover their own wings.

Then, just in time, I stopped
the cat from climbing the trunk
to challenge their squawking.
She was young, unafraid,
no, untried
in how easily harm may come –

A false step on a cliff
that refuses to release
its grasp of winter.
Sometimes the season
arrives too early,
sticks around too long.

Silence seems right
even in the coming darkness
when dreams will take
all of us, young and old,
in a snakedance
up the mountainside, with only
avalanches to carry us home.

STEPS INTO SPRING

In the valley
the tree trunks are twisted
with age. All that they know
has been tattooed
into their barks, leaving
no space for the future.
Their brittle limbs
can hardly be expected
to flower.

I wind my body
in and out among them
tirelessly
dance on their roots
hoping to leave behind
an old skin.

AFRICAN CHILD

When my grandfather fell from waking
he would enter

a world of savannas and chants
where the dead walked

protecting the living,
where people sat, their bodies still

not rushing into the void of the future
but letting time seek them out

where roast ox was eaten
as food for the dead

and thorn branches piled on the graves
to keep witches at bay.

On his feet, Grandpa Butler
would not remember the dream

not even when the heavy rains came
and he and the others retreated indoors

shocked at the small white children
who splashed about in the mud

refusing to return the world
to the gods

who wished to work
undisturbed.

BALLET THROUGH ENCROACHING BLINDNESS

1. *Les Rendezvous*

A tall white gate leading out of the park,
A motion in yellow-flecked white.

Cubist lines dissect, double.
Shadows blur edges, cancel out space.

The circle winds and closes,
Opens and winds. Form and space converge.

The faces,
Klee figures multiplied.

A tall white entrance to nowhere.
A motion behind the eyes, dull mustard.

2. *Airs*

No program notes. Simply
orange apparel, skins of plants.

Bare chests burst out
from the dance. Fire-sticks spring

and bounce. We place heads
from memory

but the legs
refuse to take root. I am bedded

in a December landscape on a line
that straddles north and south.

3. *Sylvia Pas de Deux*

A white sea creeps below
the monochromatic horizon.

A white spray dances in a breeze
like two figures meeting

and separating, configurations
of indigo light becoming

ocean air. When they ease
between overlapping curtain halves

to acknowledge the applause,
they are vulnerable skybirds

grounded and halved against
a world of bleeding clay.

4. *La Bayadere (The Temple-Dancer)*

Out of the forest night they wind. Robot
limbs push and droop, push and droop.

A haze of sulfur rises
to take the shape of the moon.

Mushrooms with fluted edges
capped by curving octopus limbs

draw arcs that assume substance,
pear-shaped, autonomous.

A thousand flaring dots
are hidden by darkness.

Coda

The intermittent clapping
is a distant rumble of thunder.

Now they cluster in patches
of three, four, seven.

Now they form rigid lines,
mermaid torso with multiple edges.

What occurs inside
is the echo of a primeval edict.

I am dismembered within the canvas,
the discipline breaking

into a fantasy night, slicing
the membrane of a virgin eye.

OUT OF A BARREN LAND

They say, there is sun
and bright green leaves and
that every now and then the rain
touches only the surfaces
of life in Florence, that the air is filled
with the high-pitched voices of children,
and tourists hug themselves with joy.

They say, more doors
have been thrown wide open
revealing forgotten courtyards and
so many artworks fading into the past
have been restored
in colors rivaling the originals.

I say, I still see
the dark-skinned beggars huddled
against stone barriers as if they
recognize a winter we all would deny
and that those who stand
entranced before the images
clutch their purses in fear of thieves.

I say, the rain comes
and still the ambulance rushes down
Via Massacio, and the voice
of the Arno's flow is drowned
by traffic noise dominating the banks.

And I say,
I will wait, I will wait
for the figure to come riding in
on a white mare
down the hills now hidden in mist

through the old city gates
congested with blaring horns, across
the river, hooves tapping
the stones surrounding the Baptistery

The figure who will ask
the question long silenced
Who is the woman depicted
standing alone
in robes of sun and sky

No longer listening to the message
of the fairhaired man
his body emerging from bright wings

no longer cuddling a baby
in the crook of an arm?

AFTER DONATELLO'S *MAGDALEN*

I have turned over
the leaves in this book
so often
that the edges
are brittle, not like
words, but like the sound
of remembered birdwings
in a desert. The curtain
that closes my face
from the eyes
that pause on the pavement
beneath my window

boasts it own torn edges
and my hair, once full
with the smell of love, clings
to my mind
begging for mercy.

SAN VITALE, BOLOGNA

The mosaics on the walls
carry the century with dignity
fading into the rust-browns
of earth. Carved out of a rock,
the chapel is a cave
of reverence, a dance to
the nymphs of the peninsula.

Only when the indoor lights
go out,
do the reds and golds
of the elongated windows
flash their abstract beauty
across the stone floor.

DAWN

I have waited long
for this day, the moment
in my life
when all would be
less tentative. This morning
the sun shines on everything
and we all know at last
that summer has come
to stay.

I too recognize
the recovered body
I will inhabit, the work
that will continue
through the years, the walls
that will enclose me,
the regrets
that never desert me.

There is comfort in this,
finally learning to maneuver
city traffic without fear,
no longer reaching for
cool lagoons, steep pinnacles.
There is peace
in early wakings like this

and only the residue
of dreams sift
now and then
through my days.

CALLED BACK

Suddenly
you are once more everywhere,
reclaiming your dreamself, as if
you were never interred,
a mother,
no longer stooped,
no longer refraining words in
the lethean flood of a weary spirit.

You walk agile
through my nightworld, your mind
quickening a house that

       once upon a time
crumbled beneath
rotten boards and sagging roofs,
now shining stained and weathered,
wood swollen and hardening
in its maturity, room
expanding to invite others in

begging them to share
what as children
we could never hold onto,
walls made way to allow motion
that will rock this secret harvest of
sorrow, site for language
that threatens to escape a fortress
of untimely gathered bricks.

Yet what surprises
is the way the mind tricks me,
how on this plateau weathered by
centuries of insistent drumming,

chants making voids for all of us
to so latterly enter, hugging
twisted souls, windswept visions

So often I lift the phone
to push my voice through canyons
to reach presences I cling to
that subsist on wetter lands
        and crouching landscapes,
to announce the pregnancy
swelling my breath
        and it is you
who darkens my soul's pulse
        you
            Madre
                Earth Mother

waiting in that village
of dead souls,
that parallel world,
for that keen that must float in
on a fragile wind
voicing how I again walk
slowly but steadily

        Home.

Marcella Taylor's poetry has appeared in numerous journals and anthologies including *Poetry, Wisconsin Review, The Eagle, Tampa Bay Review, Ragmag* and *Embers* and in two volumes of poetry, *The Lost Daughter* and *Songs for the Arawak.* She has received awards, grants and residencies from The Jerome Foundation, The Carmargo Foundation, The Michener Foundation, The Loft, SASE, The Fulbright Foundation, Ragdale, Norcroft, and The Helene Wurlitzer Foundation of New Mexico. She has taught Creative Writing at St. Olaf College and at other institutions and conferences. She was born in the Bahamas of Scottish, African, French, Cherokee and Irish ancestry but has spent most of her adult life in Minnesota.